WINTER
ACTIVITY BOOK

Clare Beaton

b small publishing

- Most projects in this book use things you will already have around your home. Just check the 'What you will need' list on each page before you start to make sure you have everything ready.
- Always take great care with sharp tools such as scissors, needles and knives.
- Always cover work surfaces with newspaper before you start to paint or use glue.
- Wash your hands and wear an apron before preparing food.

Some basic tools and materials:
paint and brushes
glue
scissors
wool and darning needle
card and paper
tracing paper and pencil

 A snowflake has drifted down on to each page. See if you can spot it as you go through the book.

Snowflakes

We get snow instead of rain in cold weather because at low temperatures water vapour in the air freezes into clusters of crystals – snowflakes.

Each one 'grows' from the centre outwards and each has six points, but they all have a unique pattern – like fingerprints – no two are the same.

When you are happy with your snowflake design, draw over it in pen. Then you can rub out the template guide lines.

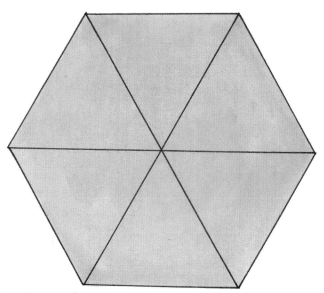

Template

Use this template as a starting point for your own snowflake design. Trace this shape on to tracing paper, then turn the paper over and scribble over the lines with a soft pencil. Turn the paper over again, tape it on to a piece of card or paper, and draw firmly over the lines again.

Tidy tray

Transform a shoe box into an attractive place to put away all the bits and pieces you've collected over the summer. You'll know where to find them for next year!

What you will need:
* shoe box
* corrugated card
* glue
* scissors
* piece of wrapping paper or wallpaper
* paints and brush
* felt tip pen

1 Measure a strip of paper long enough to wrap around the box, and add 2 cm. Make the strip 5 cm higher than the sides of the box. Cut it out.

2 Starting from a corner, stick the paper around the box leaving an overlap top and bottom. Fold over the edges of the paper and glue down.

3 Cut a piece of card to fit in the box, and about 10-15 cm taller. Draw a design on it and cut around the top of the shape.

4 Paint your design in bright colours. When it is dry, glue the card inside the box.

Recycle your old Christmas and birthday cards, postcards and photographs. Use them to create decorations of all shapes and sizes. The templates on the page opposite will help.

What you will need:
❋ wool
❋ large darning needle
❋ cards of all types
❋ scissors
❋ glue
❋ hole punch

Cut out pictures or photos and glue them on to coloured card of different shapes (see opposite page).

To make a new greetings card, cut two pieces the same shape and sew around their edges. Stitch them together along one edge, as shown below.

Use the darning needle and wool to sew around the edges of the card. Make stitches 5 mm from the edge and 5 mm apart. Use long pieces of wool so you don't have to tie on new pieces very often.

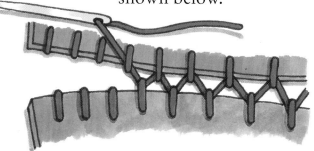

Mini-tassels

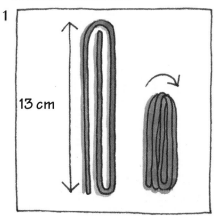

1

13 cm

Fold wool in three. Fold the bundle in half.

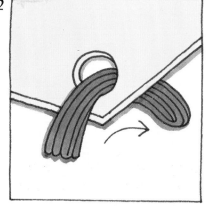

2

Push the folded end of the wool through a hole.

3

Pass the ends through the folded loop and pull firmly. Cut the ends off straight.

snowflake

triangle

star

Templates

Trace a shape on to tracing paper. Turn over and scribble over the shape with a soft pencil. Turn over again, place on card and draw firmly over the shape outline again. Remove the tracing paper and cut out the shape.

Don't trim the top loop, use it to hang your decoration.

Here are some ideas for using the templates, mini-tassels and stitching

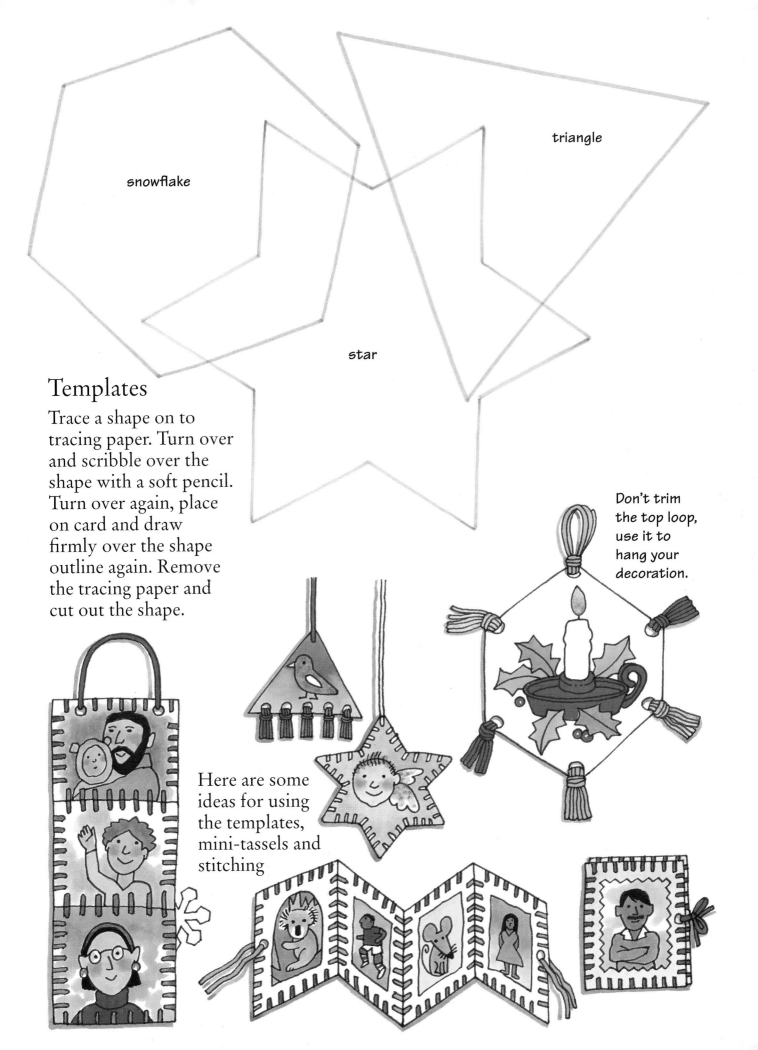

Find a flat surface to play on and tape a cup on its side at each end of the 'playing field', about 50 cm apart. If you don't have a ball you can make one by scrunching up a piece of paper and wrapping it in sticky tape.

What you will need:
* ✳ 2 straws
* ✳ 2 paper or plastic cups
* ✳ sticky tape
* ✳ small light ball
  (e.g. ping pong ball)

Paint your cup in your favourite club colours

How to play
Place the ball in the centre of the pitch. At the signal each player tries to get a goal by blowing the ball towards their cup using a straw. The player who scores the most goals wins the match.

You can introduce as many real football rules as you like, for example changing ends at half time, taking penalty 'kicks', and so on.
If you run out of puff you can flick the ball with your finger.

Paper mosaics

Create a picture with small pieces of paper glued down on a card background.

What you will need:
* ❋ old magazines
* ❋ glue
* ❋ piece of card
* ❋ scissors
* ❋ pencil

Cut or tear different coloured papers into small pieces. Keep them in small piles of the same colour.

Draw a simple picture. Colour your drawing by sticking the small pieces of paper on it.

You could use coloured sticky shapes for the eyes.

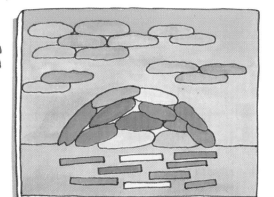

For wintery scenes use cool colours such as blues and greys.
For warmer scenes use warm colours such as yellows, oranges and reds.

Combine cut and torn pieces of paper.

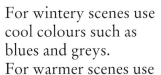

You could make a border around your picture with silver or coloured papers.

Use different shades of the same colours to create a beautiful sunset over the sea, for example.

Make yourself a papier maché piggy bank and use the winter to start saving!

What you will need:
- ❊ balloon
- ❊ wallpaper paste
- ❊ old newspapers
- ❊ egg box
- ❊ sticky tape
- ❊ 2 plastic bowls
- ❊ wooden spoon
- ❊ thin card
- ❊ vaseline
- ❊ paint and brush
- ❊ craft knife

1

Blow up a balloon (not too full) and smear it all over with vaseline.

2

Tear up the newspaper into smallish strips and put into one of the bowls.

3

Mix up the wallpaper paste in the other bowl, following the instructions on the packet.

4

Stick the paper strips on to the balloon leaving the knot sticking out. Cover with several layers. Smooth down as you go along. Leave to dry.

5

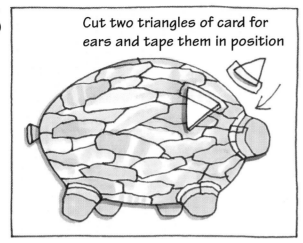

Cut two triangles of card for ears and tape them in position

Cut four legs and a snout from the egg box. Tape them in position.

6

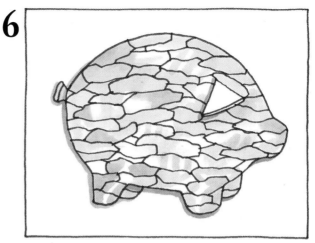

Cover the legs, snout and ears with paper until they are firmly attached.

7

Take care when using a craft knife

When the pig is completely dry, pop the balloon near the knot and pull it out. Paper over the hole. Carefully cut a slot in the top with a craft knife.

8

Paint your pig in bright colours. Add eyes, a tail, and a smile!

SAVING TIPS

Think of something to save for, like:
- a holiday
- a special treat
- Christmas

Try and put a regular amount into piggy each week

Earn a little money doing jobs at home

Every penny counts!

Pom-poms

Decorate your clothes and hair with these jolly woollen balls. Alter the size by using different-sized rings or by varying the thickness of the wool.

What you will need:

❋ wool
❋ thin card
❋ pair of compasses
❋ scissors
❋ darning needle

1

Draw a circle 3 cm across on a piece of card. Using the same centre point, draw another circle measuring 8 cm.

2

Cut out the ring and make a second one by drawing around the first. Place the two together.

3

Start winding wool around the rings. Continue until the central hole is filled in.

4

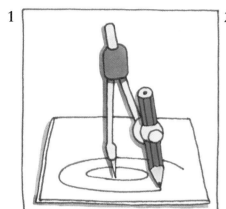

Push the point of the scissors between the wool and the two card rings. Cut the wool around the ring.

5

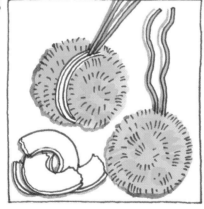

Push a 30 cm length of wool between the rings and tie tightly in a knot. Tear off the card rings and fluff out your pom-pom.

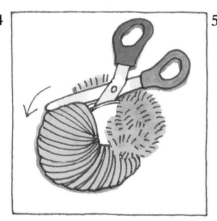

Tie on to hair bands of all kinds.

Use a darning needle to sew on to hats and scarves.

These tassels will brighten up all kinds of things, from bags to cushions. Make multi-coloured ones, or make larger ones by lengthening the piece of card, or mini ones by shortening the card.

What you will need:
* ❋ wool
* ❋ card
* ❋ ruler and pencil
* ❋ scissors
* ❋ darning needle

1

For a tassel 10 cm long, cut a piece of card 12 cm x 7 cm.

2

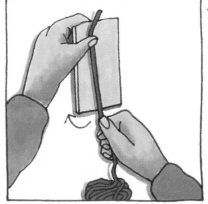

Wind wool around the card at least 20 times. The more times, the fatter the tassel.

3

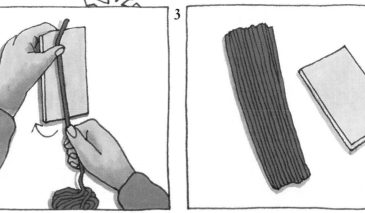

Cut the wool along one edge of the card. Open the wool carefully and lie it out flat.

4

Lay a 40 cm length of wool on top. Tie around the middle tightly with another piece of wool.

5

Fold the bundle in two, with the long piece of wool coming out of the top.

6

Wind a 20 cm length of wool around the top of the tassel and knot tightly. Trim the bottom if necessary.

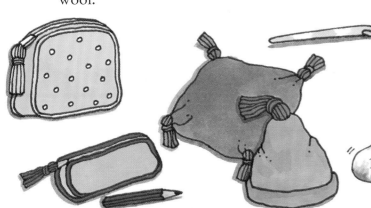

Use a darning needle to sew your tassels on to jumpers, cushions, hats and scarves.

Long ago winters were very hard in the Northern Hemisphere and many ancient festivals were to encourage the sun to regain its strength. As the weather was bad and the days were short, people had a long break from their farming and time to celebrate and look forward to warmer weather. Other traditional winter festivals celebrate the end of one year and the start of the next.

Christmas

This is the Christian celebration of the birth of Jesus Christ on December 25th. In churches and homes people put a 'crib', a model of the scene of the birth of baby Jesus in a stable. It shows Jesus's parents, Mary and Joseph, the three kings and shepherds who came to see the baby, and all the animals.

People also decorate the streets with lights and put a decorated fir tree in their homes. Families have a special meal together, either on Christmas Day or on Christmas Eve.

Chanukah

This is an eight-day festival in December when Jews celebrate the miracle of the lamp full of holy oil that burned for eight days, over 2000 years ago. They light one candle each day on a special eight-branched candlestick called a 'menorah'. Families have parties and eat potato pancakes called 'latkes'. Children receive small gifts on each of the eight days of the festival.

Id-ul-Fitr

This is the three-day Muslim festival to celebrate the end of Ramadan, the holy month. During Ramadan, Muslims have to fast (not eat) from sunrise until sunset. At Id people can eat when they want and there are special cakes, biscuits and sweets. They give money to the poor and send cards. The festival starts in December or January when the new moon is first spotted in the sky.

Snow houses

Press out the igloo and châlet. Fold them carefully along the dotted lines and glue together on the flaps where shown. You can use the châlet as a box with an opening roof.

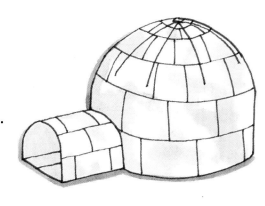

Igloo

In northern Canada the Inuit people keep warm in houses made from blocks of ice!

Igloo tunnel

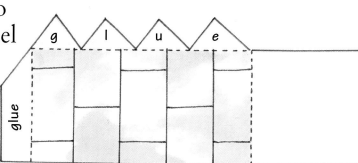

g l u e

glue

Châlet roof

Press out. Fold a crease along the dotted line.

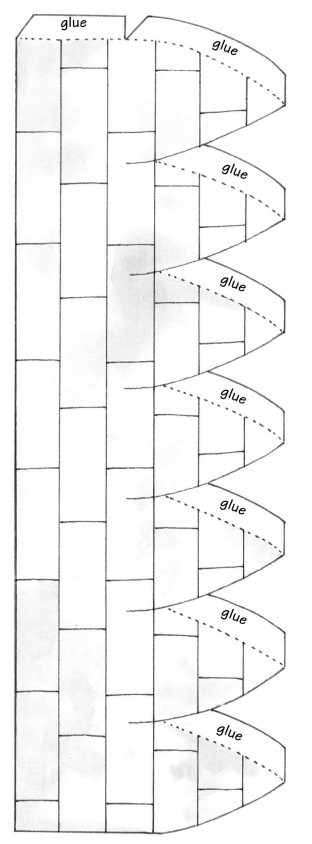

glue
glue
glue
glue
glue
glue
glue
glue

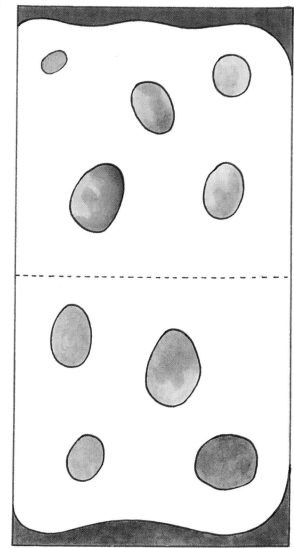

Châlet

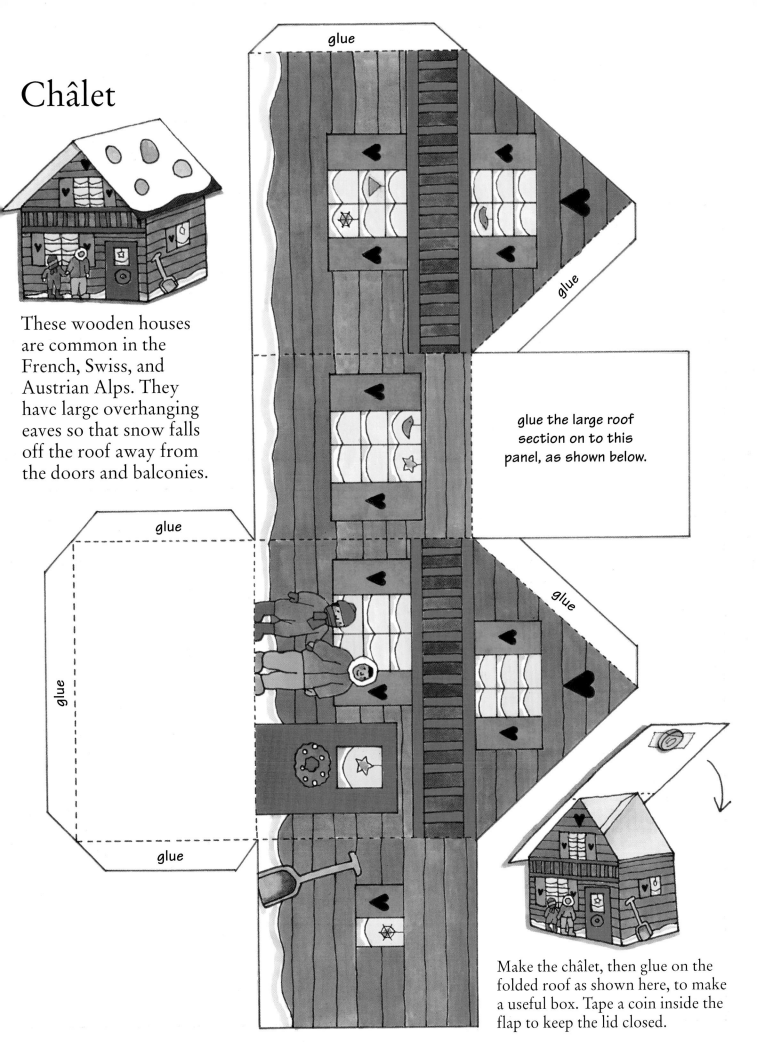

These wooden houses are common in the French, Swiss, and Austrian Alps. They have large overhanging eaves so that snow falls off the roof away from the doors and balconies.

glue

glue

glue the large roof section on to this panel, as shown below.

glue

glue

glue

glue

glue

Make the châlet, then glue on the folded roof as shown here, to make a useful box. Tape a coin inside the flap to keep the lid closed.

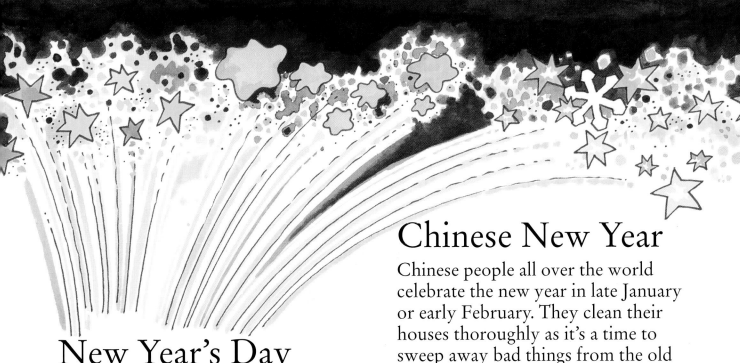

Chinese New Year

Chinese people all over the world celebrate the new year in late January or early February. They clean their houses thoroughly as it's a time to sweep away bad things from the old year. The special new year colours are red for good luck and gold for plenty. Huge dragons lead street processions and people let off fireworks.

New Year's Day

This is the 1st January, the start of the new year. The night before, on New Year's Eve, people celebrate with parties. At the stroke of midnight they drink a toast, kiss each other, and often make a lot of noise with singing and fireworks. If you make a 'new year's resolution' you try and break a bad habit or start a good one in the year to come.

St. Valentine's Day

On 14th February, people celebrate love. They send cards decorated with hearts to those they love, unsigned, so their love is kept secret.

On February 15th, in an ancient Roman festival, young men chose a girl by pulling names out of a big jar. Is this the origin of St Valentine's Day?

These are best eaten straight away, warm from the oven, but they will keep for up to a week in an airtight tin. Makes about 12.

 You could also try making letters or numbers

What you will need
* ❋ 1 envelope dried yeast
* ❋ 4 tablespoons warm water
* ❋ 1 tablespoon golden syrup
* ❋ 1 teaspoon each of salt and sea salt
* ❋ 175 g whole wheat flour
* ❋ 1 beaten egg, and a brush
* ❋ mixing bowl and wooden spoon
* ❋ baking tray

1

Preheat the oven to 425°F/220°C or gas mark 7. In the mixing bowl, dissolve the yeast in the warm water.

2

Add the syrup and salt (not sea salt). Mix well. Stir in the flour. Knead the dough on a floured surface.

3

Roll the dough into snakes. Form into pretzel shapes (twists) and place on baking tray.

4

Brush with egg and sprinkle with sea salt. Cook in the centre of the oven for about 10 minutes. Take care – the oven will be hot!

Chocolate fudge

Really delicious, and very quick and easy to make. Give some as a present.

What you will need
* ❋ 100 g plain chocolate
* ❋ 50 g butter
* ❋ 3 tablespoons single cream
* ❋ 1 teaspoon vanilla essence
* ❋ 450 g icing sugar
* ❋ small saucepan and bowl
* ❋ wooden spoon and sieve
* ❋ 20 cm square baking tin

1

Take care!
Ask an adult to help.

Break up the chocolate and put into the bowl with the butter. Place over a saucepan of simmering water, stirring occasionally.

2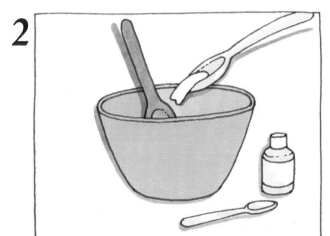

When melted, turn off the heat and remove the bowl from the saucepan. Stir in the cream and vanilla essence.

3

Slowly add the sieved icing sugar, mixing well until thick and chocolatey.

4

Butter the baking tin and press the fudge into it. Cool it in the fridge until it is set firm. Cut it into pieces.

Fleece hat and scarf

Fleece is wonderfully easy to work with. It is stretchy, doesn't fray when cut, and doesn't have a 'wrong' side. You can leave your hat and scarf plain or decorate them using the ideas on the page opposite.

What you will need:
* ⅓ metre fleece, 150cm wide (60")
* sewing machine or needle and thread
* tracing paper
* pencil
* scissors
* pins

Guide for cutting out

1
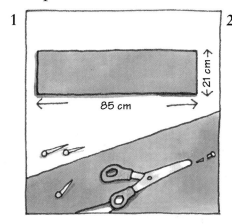
Lay out the fabric on a flat surface. Measure out the scarf and mark with pins. Cut out.

2

Trace the hat template on to tracing paper. Pin to the bottom edge of the fabric.

3
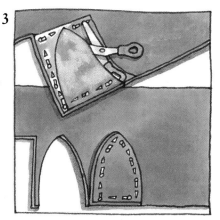
Cut through the paper and fleece. Cut another three using the first one.

4
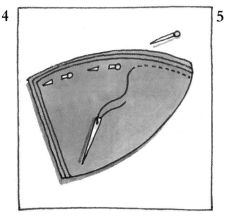
Pin the curved edges of two pieces together and sew together 5 mm from the edge.

5
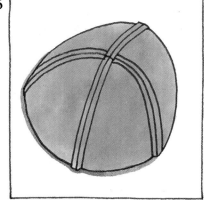
Attach the remaining three pieces in the same way, to form a domed shape.

6
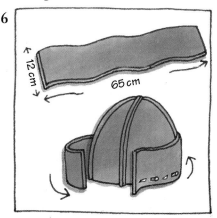
Cut a strip 12 cm x 65 cm from the remaining fleece. Pin it around the bottom of the hat. Start at a hat seam and leave 10mm of the strip sticking out at the beginning.

7

Sew the strip to the hat 5 mm in from the bottom edge. Sew the ends of the strip together and trim the ends if necessary.

8
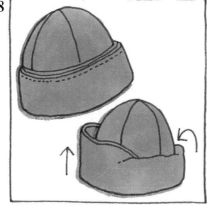

Turn right-side out. Fold the strip up over the hat and tuck in the top edge to form a thick band.

Decoration

Decorate the band of the hat (sewing through the two layers), and the ends of the scarf. Remember that your stitching will show on both sides of the scarf. To make pompoms and tassels, see pages 10 and 11.

Wool stitching

Use coloured wool and a darning needle to decorate your hat and scarf with simple stitching.

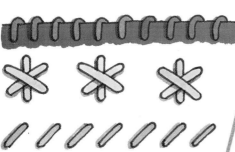

Buttons

You could sew a row of buttons for decoration. Sew buttons on each side of the scarf in the same position.

Hat template

Snow storm

Use small jars such as baby food jars, with good screw-top lids. Clean and dry them and remove all labels. When you choose the toy make sure it fits nicely in the jar. It must have a flat base for gluing, and remember the bottom will be hidden by the lid.

What you will need:
❋ small glass jar
❋ baby oil
❋ glitter or small sequins
❋ small toy or decoration
❋ glue

1

Carefully fill the jar with the oil.

2

Add some glitter or small sequins (or both!) to the oil.

3

Glue the small toy to the centre inside of the lid. Add glue around the inside edge of the lid then screw it tightly on to the jar.

4

Leave time for the glue to dry. Then turn the jar upside down and give it a shake. Watch the 'snow' swirling.

For most creatures winter is a hard time to find food and keep warm and dry. Some hibernate (go into a deep sleep) and some migrate to warmer countries for the winter months. However there are some animals who have adapted to survive winter in the Arctic, the coldest time in the coldest part of the world. Some fish and plants have also adapted so they can live in these harsh conditions.

Reindeer

These remarkably hardy animals live in the Arctic. Their thick waterproof coats keep them warm even in blizzards. They have hooves with a sharp cutting edge to dig through snow and ice for lichen to eat.

Musk ox

Musk ox have a fantastic woolly coat to protect them from the most severe cold. It has an undercoat of dense wool and an outer coat of long hair reaching almost to the ground.

Polar bear

The bears have a dense furry winter coat and a layer of fat up to 10 cm thick to keep them warm. Their creamy white fur is good camouflage in the snow, and it repels water to keep them dry. They have no eyelashes because they would freeze, and a third eyelid protects them from snow blindness caused by bright reflections bouncing off the snow.

Female polar bears have their cubs in a snow den in December or January and don't bring them out until March, when it's warmer.

Warming drinks

Hot spiced milk

for **4** people

What you will need:
✳ 750 ml milk
✳ 2 level tablespoons black treacle
✳ small pot double cream
✳ ground cinnamon
✳ saucepan, spoon, and 4 mugs

1 Take care! Ask an adult to help.

2

3

Put the milk and treacle into the saucepan and warm gently.

Pour into four mugs. Stir briskly, then pour the cream over the back of the spoon into each mug.

Sprinkle lightly with cinnamon.

Chocolate marshmallow floats

What you will need:
✳ 750 ml milk
✳ 2 heaped tablespoons drinking chocolate
✳ 8 marshmallows
✳ saucepan and 4 mugs
✳ whisk or fork

1 Take care! Ask an adult to help.

2

3

Pour the milk into the saucepan and heat gently. Remove from the heat.

Add the drinking chocolate to the milk. Whisk.

Pour into four mugs. Float two marshmallows on top of each drink.

Spot the difference

Can you spot ten differences between these two pictures?

Here are a few games to play indoors
when it's too cold and wet to play outside.

Wari

For 2 players

What you will need:

❄ 2 egg boxes
❄ 2 jar lids
❄ piece of card
❄ glue and scissors
❄ 48 dried beans or other small items
❄ paint or pens

1

Cut the lids off the egg boxes.
Glue the bases side by side in
the centre of the card.

2

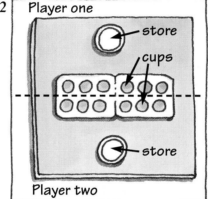

Player one · store · cups · store · Player two

Glue the two jar lids
upside-down on to the card,
one on either side of the
boxes. These are the 'stores'.

3

Cut the card into a nice
shape. Paint and decorate
the board in bright colours.

How to play

❄ Each player has 24 beans. A player
sits either side of the board and
puts 4 beans into *each* of the cups
on his side.

❄ The first player takes the 4 beans
out of any cup on his side and,
going anti-clockwise, places 1 bean
in the next cup along, until they
are finished. You can go round
to the other player's side.

❄ The second player then takes 4
beans out of one of his cups and
moves along anti-clockwise, in
the same way.

❄ Whenever a player's *last* bean falls
into an opponent's cup so that the
total number of beans in the cup is
2 or 3 he takes these, plus any 2s or
3s in the cup *immediately* before it,
and puts them all in his store.

❄ The game carries on until no more
beans can be taken. Any beans left
belong to the player whose side
they are on.

❄ The player with the most beans
in his store wins.

22

Dice games

*For 2 or more players, or
on your own against the clock!*

Strike midnight

What you will need:
* 2 dice
* paper and pencils

How to play
* Each player draws a circle for a clockface on their piece of paper.
* The object of the game is to fill in the numbers on your clockface in order, starting with 1 and ending with 12.
* Take turns to throw one die. When you get 1, write it on to your clockface in the correct position. Continue taking it in turns to throw.
* When you reach 6, start throwing both dice and adding the two numbers together.
* The winner is the first person to reach midnight.

Lucky numbers

What you will need:
* 2 dice

How to play
* Each player chooses a lucky number between 2 and 12.
* Take turns to throw the dice and add up the total showing.
* The winner is the player who throws their lucky number the most times in 10 or 20 turns.

The faster you play the quicker you have to add up!

Winter rhymes and jokes

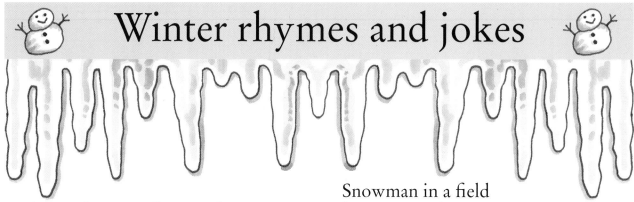

Spring is showery, flowery, bowery;
Summer is hoppy, croppy, poppy;
Autumn is slippy, drippy, nippy;
Winter is wheezy, sneezy, freezy.

Anon.

The north wind doth blow,
And we shall have snow,
And what will the robin do then,
        poor thing?
He'll sit in the barn,
And keep himself warm,
And hide his head under his wing,
        poor thing!

Anon.

Snowman in a field
listening to the raindrops
Wishing him farewell.

a Japanese haiku.

 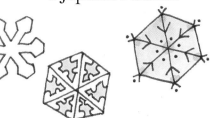

What do you call a sunburned
snowman?
Water.

What story do snowmen like to tell
their children?
Coldilocks and the three brrrs.

Knock, knock.
Who's there?
Lettuce.
Lettuce who?
Lettuce in, it's cold out here!

What do snowmen eat for breakfast?
SNOWflakes.

Published by b small publishing, Pinewood, 3a Coombe Ridings, Kingston upon Thames, Surrey KT2 7JT
© b small publishing, 2000
2 3 4 5
All rights reserved.
Design: Lone Morton *Editorial*: Catherine Bruzzone and Olivia Norton *Production*: Grahame Griffiths and Olivia Norton
No reproduction, copy or transmission of this publication may be made without written permission.
No part of this publication may be reproduced, stored in a retrieval system, or transmitted in any form or by any means, electronic,
mechanical, photocopying, recording or otherwise, without the prior permission of the publisher.
Colour reproduction: Vimnice International Ltd., Hong Kong. *Printed in China* by WKT Co. Ltd.
ISBN 1 874735 24 7
British Library Cataloguing-in-Publication Data. A catalogue record for this book is available from the British Library.

24